MICROECONOMIC DIARIES

SCHOOL GOERS EDITION

HRIDAY SHARMA

Chennai • Bangalore

CLEVER FOX PUBLISHING
Chennai, India

Published by CLEVER FOX PUBLISHING 2026

Paperback ISBN: 978-93-7500-534-6
Hardback ISBN: 978-93-7500-073-0

CONTENTS

INTRODUCTION TO MICROECONOMIC DIARIES

Does "microeconomics" sound like one of those buzzwords you just want to escape from? Like... something grown-ups say in serious meetings while you're wondering when the snacks will arrive?

Trust me, I felt the same way until I realised that microeconomics is literally happening around us all the time. Hey there! I'm Mr Oinkilibrium. Come along, let's figure out what this economics thing is really about, with a pinch of fun and a dash of real life.

ECONOMICS—Not Just a Word, But a Whole World in 9 Letters

E — Entrepreneurship (the courage to start something new)

C — Consumption (spending your money, hopefully on the right things)

O — Ownership (or Outsmarting expenses through smart savings)

N — Negotiation (ever tried bargaining with your sibling? Same skill.)

O — Opportunities to grow (they're everywhere, trust me)

M — Markets (places where buying & selling happen — not just on apps)

I — Investing wisely (whether it's your time, money, or energy)

C — Capital (money + ideas = magic)

S — Sustainability (because the future matters too)

Economics is like the rulebook of choices. It's the study of how people, businesses, and governments make decisions when their resources are limited but their wants are unlimited. Whether it's choosing what to buy, how much to produce, or how to price a product, economics helps explain the "why" behind every choice.

To put that in a more formal definition:

"Economics is the social science that studies how individuals, businesses, and societies allocate scarce resources to satisfy unlimited wants."

(Definition adapted from standard economic texts like Mankiw's Principles of Economics)

So, whether you're saving your pocket money or running a giant company, economics is all about asking:

"How do I use what I have… to get what I need… without wasting what matters?"

Why a Microeconomic Diary?

Microeconomics is a part of economics that deals with small-scale decisions–the ones made by individuals, families, and businesses. It's the side of economics that explains:

- Why you might buy chocolate today or save for a bigger gift later.
- Why does your favourite café raise prices during exam week when students flood in?
- Why does your school canteen suddenly switch snack brands to cut costs or meet demand?

Microeconomics helps us understand things like pricing, demand and supply, competition, and consumer choices.

What exactly is a microeconomic diary?

A Microeconomic Diary is a way of observing and reflecting on these small decisions. Instead of just reading about economics in textbooks, I wanted to capture it in real life, as something alive and happening.

This diary is:

- About spotting day-to-day economic choices in markets, homes, classrooms, and cafés.
- A space where I turn these moments into simple stories, comic strips, and reflections.
- A creative effort to make economics personal, relatable, and fun to learn.

Through this diary, I hope to show that microeconomics isn't some distant, complicated subject. It's in the little decisions we make and the choices that shape how we spend, save, earn, and live.

So as you flip through these pages, maybe you'll start seeing microeconomics in your own life too. And instead of running away from it, you'll say,

"Hey, that makes sense."

THAT'S OUR
DEPARTMENT OF
MICROECONCOMICS
?

DECISIONS IN ACTION

When most people hear the word "microeconomics", they immediately picture graphs, complicated equations, and maybe a few yawns. But what if I told you that microeconomics is happening every time you choose between two snacks, bargain at your local market, or wonder why your favourite app suddenly raised its subscription price?

At its core, microeconomics is the part of economics that studies individuals, households, and businesses and focuses on how they make decisions with the limited resources they have. These are decisions that involve all of us, whether we realize it or not.

But what kind of decisions are we talking about?

- Why does a school stationery shop suddenly put up a "Back to School" discount?
- Why did my favourite online game charge extra for special features this month?
- Why do small roadside vendors sometimes sell lemonade for ₹10 on normal days and ₹15 on a hot, crowded day?

- Why do I sometimes save my pocket money instead of spending it all on the weekend?

These aren't random decisions; they are microeconomic choices. They reflect things like supply, demand, consumer preferences, production costs, and competition.

Why does understanding this matter?

Because the small choices we make as individuals, and the decisions businesses make in response, build up to create larger economic trends. Understanding microeconomics helps us understand:

- How prices change and why affordability matters.
- Why businesses compete or collaborate.
- How consumers (that's us!) influence what gets sold in the market.
- How saving, spending, and investing shape our futures.

If we all start to understand the reasoning behind these choices, we won't just be better at managing our own money or making smart purchases; we'll understand how the world around us functions on a deeper level.

Now, let's take a small, everyday example where economic concepts play out in ways we usually miss:

In my school canteen, there was a time when they stopped selling one popular snack because prices from the supplier increased. Students complained, demand dropped for other snacks, and soon the canteen had to rethink their choices. That's supply and demand, along with consumer preferences in action.

Another time, during a local festival, shops around my neighbourhood raised their prices slightly because more people were buying decorations and sweets. That's seasonal price fluctuation and business strategy.

Even at home, when I save my birthday money instead of spending it all at once, that's an opportunity cost — I'm giving up today's fun for something bigger tomorrow.

Through this diary, I want to help more children, students, and even adults see that economics isn't something far away. It's right here, in our daily choices.

I hope it makes you think about:

- What makes you buy what you buy?
- Why do prices change?
- How do sellers attract customers?
- How can we all make smarter economic decisions in our daily lives?

If this booklet helps even one person smile, reflect, and understand their world a little better, I'll call this project a success.

Because in the end, microeconomics is just the study of how people, like you and me, try to make the best of what they have.

PROFIT AND LOSS

It all started with a packet of chips and a very ambitious plan. During lunch break, my friend Aryan decided to open a "mini tuck shop" from his backpack. He bought a family pack of chips for ₹100, divided it into small ziplock bags, and started selling each for ₹15.

It was going great... until someone asked, "Wait, how many did you sell?"

He counted. "Six." We did the maths.

₹15 × 6 = ₹90.

He spent ₹100. He made ₹90.

He stared at his last ₹15 bag and whispered, *"I've been betrayed by maths."*

That day, we didn't see any profit in the snacks business, but rather, unfortunately, we learnt about loss.

At its core:

Profit is what you earn when your selling price is more than your cost price.

Loss is what you face when your cost price is more than your selling price.

In simple terms:

$$\textit{Profit} = \textit{Selling Price} - \textit{Cost Price}$$
$$\textit{Loss} = \textit{Cost Price} - \textit{Selling Price}$$

It's a concept so basic that even your lemonade stand or school canteen is using it without calling it "microeconomics".

Situational Examples of Profit and Loss – a High Schooler's Life Edition:

Situation 1: You buy 5 friendship bands for ₹50 and sell each for ₹15 to your classmates who forgot to get one.

You earn ₹75. The cost was ₹50. You made a profit of ₹25.

(Who knew friendship could be profitable too?)

Situation 2: You spend ₹200 printing 20 custom bookmarks for a school event but only sell 10 at ₹15 each.

You earn ₹150. The cost was ₹200. That's a loss of ₹50.

(Lesson learned: Know your audience to assess the risks and avoid losses!)

Situation 3: You host a small bake sale and spend ₹500 on ingredients.

You earn ₹750 in total sales. The cost was ₹500. That's a profit of ₹250.

(Plus, you got compliments on your cookies … emotional profit?)

Situation 4: You and a friend invest in handmade greeting cards. You spend ₹300, and she spends ₹300.

You make ₹800 total. You split the earnings 50-50.

Joint profit: ₹200. Split: ₹100 each.

(Teamwork + math = success!)

Situation 5: You buy a concert ticket for ₹1,200 but can't go. You resell it for ₹1,000.

Loss = ₹200.

(Sometimes profit isn't possible — but it's still better than nothing. Hedge your losses!)

Every decision we make, whether it's selling snacks or reselling old books, teaches us a little more about how value works.

Profit and loss aren't just about money. They're about choices, risk, timing, and a bit of hustle.

We often think of profit and loss as just accounting terms, numbers in green and red. But in microeconomics, they're way more than that. They reflect and are the end result of decisions taken, incentives given, risks taken, opportunity costs, and even human psychology.

Profit happens when the reward is greater than the cost.

Loss happens when what you gain doesn't match up to what you gave up.

But in real life, it's rarely that simple. This is where cost-benefit analysis (CBA) steps in, one of the most useful tools in microeconomics.

WHAT IS COST-BENEFIT ANALYSIS (CBA)?

In microeconomics, cost-benefit analysis is used to evaluate whether a decision is rational from an economic standpoint. In simple terms, it's asking:

"Is what I'm getting worth what I'm giving up?"

CBA doesn't just apply to big business or government projects; it's everywhere. And the best part? The benefit isn't always monetary it can also be factors like social well-being, environmental impact, or improvements to working conditions, which are assessed using non-monetary indicators.

A few examples of applying CBA:

1. The Bandra-Worli Sea Link, Mumbai

Before construction began, planners ran a full CBA. The bridge would cost a massive amount of public money, but the social and environmental benefits of reduced fuel usage and travel time and increased connectivity were projected to outweigh the cost of construction and maintenance.

Result: It got built. And today, it saves lakhs of hours annually in travel time.

2. Buying That ₹6,000 Jacket

It looks great. But will you wear it more than twice?

CBA kicks in silently: "How many times will I wear this?" "Will I feel confident in it?" "Is this a 'style investment' or a one-day wonder?"

Microeconomically, this is consumer choice theory in action, where you are making the purchasing decision after weighing satisfaction (utility) against the cost of the jacket to help you decide if paying ₹6,000 for the jacket is worth it.

3. Students Skipping Tuition for a Hobby Class

Spending ₹1,000 on pottery instead of math coaching may look like a "loss" on the report card. But if the pottery class reduces stress and sparks creativity, the psychological return on investment might actually be higher.

This is where non-monetary utility enters microeconomic analysis.

What This Really Tells Us

Microeconomics teaches that every decision involves trade-offs. What matters most is understanding what you value and using that to guide your choices.

And that's the real goal of this diary, not just to recognise profit and loss on paper, but to ask: what did I gain? What did I give up? Was it worth it?

INFLATION

You walk into the school canteen with ₹50, confident you'll get your usual samosa and juice combo. But surprise, the samosa is now ₹20, and the juice? ₹35.

Your lunch plan just got inflated.

In microeconomics, inflation is the rise in the general price level of goods and services over time — meaning your money buys less than it used to.

It's not just a textbook term — it hits everyday choices, one price tag at a time.

Where Inflation Sneaks into Your Life:

- Canteen Confusion: The chips packet that was ₹20 last semester is now ₹25 and smaller. You're not imagining it. It's called "shrinkflation": less product, same or higher price.

- Tuition Fee Trouble: Your coaching class increases its monthly fees "to adjust for rising costs". You're paying more but learning the same.
- Pocket Money Panic: What you could once buy with ₹500 now needs ₹600.

But your parents haven't increased your allowance, thanks to inflation.

Microeconomic Angle:

Inflation doesn't just raise prices; it alters consumer behaviour:

- You start cutting back on non-essentials.
- You compare more before buying.
- You prioritise differently. Maybe skipping the cold coffee to save for a concert ticket

It also impacts producers who face rising costs for ingredients, packaging, and electricity, all of which get passed on to you, the buyer.

This is how inflation disrupts individual decision-making and resource allocation, both key pillars of microeconomics.

In economics, inflation is when prices rise and the purchasing power of money falls.

To put it simply: you need more money to buy less stuff.

Like balloons, money inflates too, except in this case, it doesn't make parties more fun.

If the price of your usual sandwich goes from ₹60 to ₹90 but your pocket money stays the same, you've just had a one-on-one with inflation.

As microeconomists would explain, inflation affects individual decision-making, consumption patterns, and real income, which is the actual value of what your money can buy, not just the number printed on the note.

The Bigger Picture: Why Inflation Hurts the System

From a microeconomic standpoint, inflation isn't just a price issue — it messes with:

1. Household Decision-Making

People stop spending on non-essentials. They postpone purchases, save less, and often prioritise survival over growth. That slows economic activity at the individual and small-business level.

2. Producers' Cost Dilemma

As the cost of inputs (like wheat, fuel, packaging) rises, businesses either increase their product prices or reduce product size — enter shrinkflation.

→ You still pay ₹20 for chips but get air and 5.5 flakes.

3. Planning & Stability

With unpredictable price hikes, both buyers and sellers lose confidence. People start hoarding goods, underinvesting, or rushing into risky alternatives just to preserve value.

Historical Glimpses — When Inflation Went Wild

1. Weimar Republic (Post WW1):

After WW1, Germany faced hyperinflation. Prices doubled every few days.

Images from the time show children building toy towers out of currency notes — not because they were rich, but because the money was worthless.

A loaf of bread went from 250 marks in January 1923 to 200 billion marks by November.

2. Venezuela and Argentina Today:

Both countries have battled inflation rates so high that prices change within hours.

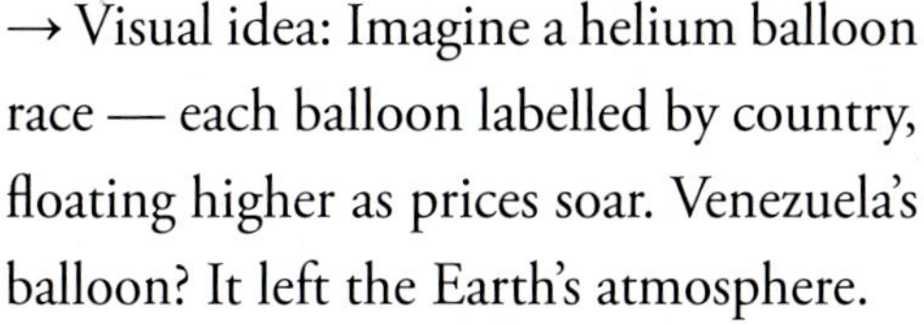

→ Visual idea: Imagine a helium balloon race — each balloon labelled by country, floating higher as prices soar. Venezuela's balloon? It left the Earth's atmosphere.

3. Zimbabwe's Legendary 50 Cent:

A meme once read: "*50 Cent in America is a rapper. 50 cents in Zimbabwe is 80 million.*"

And no, that's not an exaggeration.

Inflation doesn't just stretch prices; it stretches patience, shrinks budgets, and tests the real worth of money in everyday life.

MARKET COMPETITION

Whether it's two stalls selling the same momos outside your school gate or three juice brands battling it out on your Insta feed—that's not just choice. That's market competition.

In microeconomics, market competition is the rivalry between sellers trying to attract the same group of buyers by offering better prices, quality, or services.

It's what pushes businesses to innovate, improve, and stay sharp or risk fading into the background.

In a healthy market, competition protects consumers from high prices and low quality.

It's why we have options and why businesses are constantly trying to win us over.

- School Fest Food Stalls: You and your friend both run lemonade stalls. You lower your price, and she adds mint leaves.
  Suddenly, there's a competition on taste *and* price. Welcome to *product differentiation.*
- Instagram Hustles: Two classmates sell handmade candles online. One starts eco-packaging, the other throws in a free sticker. They're both trying to build *brand loyalty,* and you're the target.
- Chips A vs Chips B: One reduces their pack size. The other keeps it the same and advertises, "More crunch, same price!"
  You're witnessing a subtle fight for your purchase through perceived value.

In economics, market structure refers to how many sellers exist in a market, how much control they have over prices, and how similar or different their products are.

This structure shapes how businesses behave, whether they innovate, copy, overcharge, or hustle to survive.

There are four main types of market competition:

1. Perfect Competition — Where No One's Special

Countless sellers. Identical products. Zero control over price.

Imagine 30 stalls selling plain cold water outside your school during summer.

- Everyone charges the same.
- No one has a brand.
- You just go to the closest one.

Many sellers, identical products. No reason innovate, just compete on lowest price.

Perfect competition is rare in real life but exists in markets like agriculture — one farmer's wheat is (almost) the same as another's.

In perfect competition, price is the boss. Innovation? Not really. There's no room for creativity when everyone's product is the same.

2. Monopolistic Competition — Where Everyone's Slightly Special

Many sellers. Slightly different products. Lots of branding and pricing freedom.

Think: juice stalls at a school fair.

- One adds chia seeds.
- One serves in mason jars.
- One calls theirs "Immunity Booster Blast™".

This is the real world of cafés, clothing brands, bakeries, and even tuition teachers — where businesses sell *almost* the same thing but work hard to differentiate.

Here, innovation thrives — because sellers need to stand out.

3. Oligopoly — The Big Boss Club

Few sellers. High control. Tough to enter.

This is where the illusion of choice kicks in.

You see 15 toothpaste brands, but most are owned by just 2 or 3 companies.

→ *Looks like freedom. Feels like control.*

"Capitalism creates competition!"

Microeconomics whispers, "Nope, *perfect competition does. Oligopolies create ads and overpriced shampoo.*"

Real-world examples:

- The soft drink industry (Coca-Cola & Pepsi own *everything*)

- Smartphones (Apple, Samsung… and a few brands trying not to cry)
- Airlines, cement, oil, telecom

Funny twist?

When YouTubers launch terrible ₹1,500 hoodies, it's bad fashion but good economics — they're cracking open the oligopoly.

4. Monopoly — One Seller to Rule Them All

One seller. No competition. Full control.

You felt it when you bought Boardwalk and Park Place in Monopoly and your friends started sweating.

That's the *monopoly.* Power. Control. Tears.

Real-life monopolies?

- Indian Railways (government-owned)
- Local electricity boards in some areas
- Pharma companies with patents (you *need* the medicine; they *own* the rights)

But monopolies can also exist in the hallway:

- Your best friend is the only one who sells *good notes* before exams.
- She sets the price. You don't argue. That's micro-level monopoly power in action.

Capitalism ≠ Innovation

People often say, "Capitalism drives innovation."

But here's the catch: true innovation comes from perfect or monopolistic competition

— where sellers must offer something better to survive.

Oligopolies and monopolies? They often just sit on their throne… until someone kicks it.

Market competition decides how many choices you *really* have — and whether your wallet benefits or your options are just an illusion.

SUPPLY AND DEMAND

Ever noticed how when *everyone* wants something, it suddenly becomes *more expensive* or *harder to get*? And when nobody wants it, shops practically beg you to take it off their shelves?

That invisible tug-of-war you just witnessed? That's demand and supply in action.

In microeconomics,

- Demand refers to how much people *want* a product and are *willing to pay* for it.
- Supply refers to how much of that product is *available* for sale.

The price of almost everything around you is determined by how demand and supply dance (or crash) together.

What It Looks Like in Real Life:

1. Limited-Edition Shoes Drop:

Only 100 pairs. 10,000 people want them. Prices skyrocket on resale apps.

Classic case of low supply + high demand = price surge.

2. Overstocked Stationery:

The school store misjudged and ordered 500 glitter pens. No one's buying them.

Supply > Demand → Prices drop to "Buy 1, Get 3."

3. Influencer Hype Flop:

A popular YouTuber launches a ₹2,000 "signature" notebook. No one buys it.

→ *High supply, zero demand.* The product quietly disappears next month.

Demand and supply don't just decide prices—they decide what's worth chasing and what's left behind.

Supply and demand aren't just boring textbook terms. They're the reason you paid ₹70 for popcorn last week and still didn't complain.

At its core, this concept is about what people want (demand) and how much of it is available (supply). And when these two don't match? Prices shift, behaviours change, and economists celebrate.

The Two Golden Laws

The Law of Supply:

As the price increases, producers are willing to make and sell more of it. Why? Because there's money to be made.

Think: When fidget spinners were cool, every shop in town stocked them. Why? High price = high profit = high supply.

The Law of Demand:

As the price increases, consumers demand less of the good. Why? Because their wallets flinch.

Think: If momos suddenly cost ₹100 for 4 pieces, even momo-lovers would pause. That's price sensitivity — also known as elasticity.

Sweet Spot Example: Mangoes in Summer

At the start of summer, mangoes are rare and expensive, demand is high, supply is low.

By mid-season, everyone's selling mangoes, so supply shoots up and prices drop. Buyers are happy, sellers feel the *aam*-burn.

This is **market equilibrium** in action. The point where supply = demand = a fair-ish price.

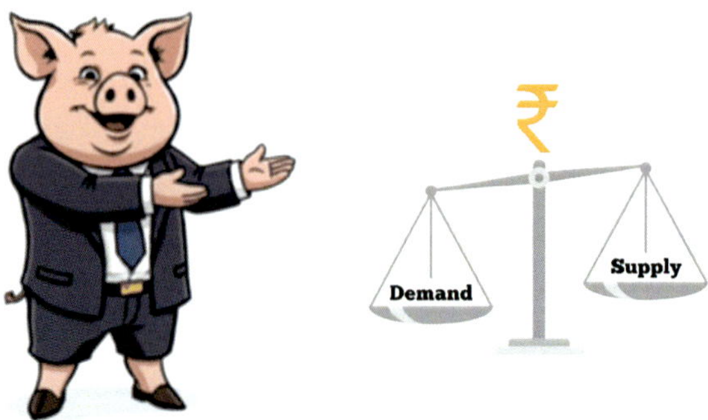

Real-Life Market Drama: The PS5 Case

When the PlayStation 5 launched, demand exploded. But Sony couldn't produce enough units.

Result? Black market prices shot up to 2x or 3x retail.

Gamers still paid.

That's inelastic demand, when people buy something even if the price is wild, just because they *need* it (or think they do).

Other Situations You Know But Didn't Realize Were Economics:

- A YouTuber drops overpriced merch everyone buys it in the first 2 days, then interest dies.
  Demand curve in reverse. First high, then flatlines.

- During cricket matches, pizza prices can double, and people still order. But moviegoers smuggle popcorn if it costs ₹300.
  Some demand is elastic (popcorn), some isn't (cricket-night pizza).
- A company overproduces "AI dog collars". No one buys them.
  Excess supply, no demand. Someone should've done a better CBA.

Let's Talk Elasticity

Elasticity measures how much demand or supply changes when something else changes — like price, income, or weather.

- During New Year's Eve, Uber surge pricing makes fares 3x.
  People still pay. That's inelastic demand — need > price pain.
- But if cafés raise cold coffee prices during winters? People skip it. That's elastic demand — price ↑, demand ↓.

Elasticity helps businesses predict behaviour, and for economists, it's like emotional intelligence for markets.

Don't Forget Opportunity Cost

Every decision has a price even if you're not paying with money.

- Netflix vs. Exams?
  You binge-watch.
  → Opportunity cost = better grade you didn't earn.
- Elon Musk building Tesla instead of buying an island?
  → Opportunity cost = coconut water and sunsets he gave up for rocket fuel.
- Indian government building statues instead of schools?
  → Opportunity cost = quality education for future voters.

Opportunity cost is a key part of CBA (Cost-Benefit Analysis) — the method that weighs if something is *worth it.*

Every price tag is a story, of who wants it, how badly, how much exists, and who's willing to pay. Demand & supply just tell that story in economic language.

CORRUPTION

We usually imagine corruption as something that happens in shady government offices or political scandals splashed across the news. But zoom in, and you'll find it creeping into smaller spaces too, including schools, homes and businesses.

From a microeconomic point of view, corruption happens when individuals use their position or power to gain unfair personal benefit, usually by bending the rules, distorting incentives, or blocking competition.

It creates inefficiency, unfair pricing, and a loss of trust in the system — whether that system is your school council, your local vendor, or your tuition class.

But what does this look like in everyday life?

Canteen Politics: A student gets their food first every day, not because they were early, but because their cousin works there. Everyone else waits. That's queue corruption — subtle, but unfair.

The "Fixed" Competition: You spend a week working on a poster for the school competition. But the winner turns out to be the judge's niece, whose entry was… meh. That's *favouritism*, and in economics, it distorts incentives. Why would you work hard next time?

Tuitions with a Twist: Your coaching teacher gives *slightly more helpful* notes to the students who take personal classes with him outside school. Others are left guessing in tests. That's *private gain at public cost.*

Backdoor Bookings: A student "borrows" a sports team slot for their friend, skipping the selection trial. That means someone who deserved it is now on the bench. That's a *resource allocation failure.*

Even if no money changes hands, these are micro-corruptions. They disrupt fairness, reduce motivation, and create a system where talent loses to access.

Corruption, even in small doses, doesn't just break rules; it breaks trust, incentives, and the invisible balance that keeps systems fair.

Corruption doesn't always come wearing a mask. Sometimes, it looks like a handshake. A favour. A shortcut.

At its core, corruption is the misuse of power for personal gain, especially in the public sector, where power is supposed to serve the people, not individuals.

From a microeconomic perspective, corruption affects the way decisions are made in households, businesses, and local systems. It doesn't just destroy fairness; rather, it actively disrupts incentives, distorts resource allocation, and weakens the foundation of trust that markets and communities depend on.

Types of Corruption and What They Mean Economically:

- *Bribery:* Offering or accepting money to break or bend the rules.
  This distorts enforcement people stop fearing consequences and start trusting loopholes.
- *Embezzlement:* Stealing or redirecting public funds meant for public services.
  This leads to poor infrastructure, underfunded schools, broken hospitals and lost opportunities.
- *Influence Peddling & Lobbying:* Using your connections to push private interests over public good.
  This restricts competition, creating a "pay-to-play" system where merit doesn't stand a chance.
- *Nepotism/Favouritism:* Giving someone an advantage because they're related or close to you.
  This breaks down incentive systems people stop trying if effort isn't rewarded fairly.

Why Does It Matter in Microeconomics?

Corruption may seem like a "big picture" problem, but its impact begins at the smallest levels.

Here's how it messes with microeconomic foundations:

1. Distorts Market Practices

Imagine two vendors competing to supply school uniforms. One offers lower prices and better quality. The other bribes the official in charge.

→ The second vendor gets the contract.

→ Students pay more. Quality suffers.

→ The honest vendor leaves the market.

This discourages competition and destroys efficiency, one transaction at a time.

2. Blocks Equal Access to Resources

In a fair system, opportunities should go to those who earn them. But when someone uses power to jump the queue or tilt the rules in their favour, scarce resources get misallocated.

That means:

- The best candidate doesn't get the scholarship.
- The hardest-working player doesn't make the team.
- The real innovator never gets funding.

This reduces social mobility and, over time, slows down economic progress.

3. Reduces Public Trust

Microeconomics assumes that people respond to incentives. But when people realize the system is rigged, that effort doesn't guarantee reward they disengage.

Why work harder if connections matter more?

Why follow rules if rule-breaking is rewarded?

This weakens market participation, lowers productivity, and feeds long-term inequality.

Why It's Hard to Notice and Easy to Ignore

The scariest thing about corruption is how normal it can start to feel.

When people around you are cutting corners or pulling strings, not doing it feels like a disadvantage. But this "everyone-does-it" attitude creates a vicious cycle. And soon, the only people losing are the ones playing fair.

Corruption isn't just illegal; it's economically irrational. It kills merit, inflates inefficiency, and robs entire communities of their right to grow.

POCKET MONEY – BUDGETING AND SPENDS

Now that we have seen Microeconomics in action in the world around us, let's see it in practice.

Suppose you get **₹1,000** as a monthly allowance. Then in March, you do some extra chores, do great in your exams, and visit a few relatives during your break all of which give you an additional **₹1,500**. Then you have a total of **₹2,500** for that month.

This is then your *income* for March.

Simply put, Income or Earnings is the total money that you get.

Now out of the **₹2500**, you immediately put **₹1,000** into your piggy bank – you are waiting to be able to buy the latest super Nerf gun!

This **₹1,000** in your piggy bank is your savings.

Simply put, Savings is the money you keep aside for future requirement.

Instead of putting this **₹1,000** in your piggy bank, you can be smart and give it to your parents instead and negotiate with them to return it to you in a month with 15% extra. You are now *Investing* **₹1,000** so that you can earn more. This 15% is the *Interest* you have earned on your investment. So at the end of April you will get back **₹1,150** instead of **₹1,000**. May is starting to look good; you have **₹150** extra already.

Banks and the Stock Market are financial institutes which help money grow – though maybe not as much as parent negotiated rates!

Simply put, Investment is putting your money where it will increase over time.

The remaining **₹1,500** you can't wait to spend - and you have the list ready. This is your budget for April.

- **₹100** on the latest pack of Football trading cards you've been eyeing
- **₹500** on the House of Candy cart in the nearby mall (Mom won't let you spend more!)
- Rs 15 on a Samosa at the school canteen whenever you feel like it
- **₹200** on 2 cool Hot wheel cars you saw in your local toy shop
- **₹750** on a cool t-Rex t-shirt

Your Spend list for the budget is ready!

Simply put, a budget is a plan of how to spend an amount of money over a particular period of time

You hurry to the shops as soon as possible and become the proud owner of the t-shirt, trading cards and candy and cars. Capitalism rocks!

Short breaks in school are also great – samosas also rock!

However, after 10 days of eating samosas in school, you realize that you spent your last bit of money for the month yesterday.

You can now either

- "Borrow" more money from your parents - not a great idea, as you're hoping they have forgotten the extra money you took in February.
- Ask your parents to return the **₹1,000** that you invested. Again, not a great idea as you really want the Nerf gun! You will then also miss out on the interest you negotiated
- Give the canteen teller an "I own you" note. Well, you tried, but got shooed away after being shown the "No Credit" sign!

So you decide to tough it out and have your next samosa next month only. After all, a Samosa is only a *Want* and not a *Need*. This thought takes you through the rest of the month in continued good spirits, till your next allowance.